A WATERY WORLD

By Emma Carlson Berne

Consultant: Beth Gambro
Reading Specialist, Yorkville, Illinois

Minneapolis, Minnesota

Teaching Tips

Before Reading

- Look at the cover of the book. Discuss the picture and the title.
- Ask readers to brainstorm a list of what they already know about underwater animals. What can they expect to see in the book?
- Go on a picture walk, looking through the pictures to discuss vocabulary and make predictions about the text.

During Reading

- Read for purpose. Encourage readers to think about animals that live under water as they are reading.
- Ask readers to look for the details of the book. What are they learning about how underwater animals get the things they need?
- If readers encounter an unknown word, ask them to look at the sounds in the word. Then, ask them to look at the rest of the page. Are there any clues to help them understand?

After Reading

- Encourage readers to pick a buddy and reread the book together.
- Ask readers to name two ways animals have adapted to life in water. Find the pages that tell about these things.
- Ask readers to write or draw something they learned about underwater animals.

Credits:
Cover and title page, © Damocean/iStock; 3, © burnsboxco/iStock; 5, © Damocean/iStock; 7, © LaSalle-Photo/iStock; 8–9, © EXTREME-PHOTOGRAPHER/iStock; 11, © mtruchon/iStock; 12–13, © vojce/iStock; 15, © cinoby/iStock; 16–17, © ultramarinfoto/iStock; 19, © PDScott/Adobe Stock; 20–21, © strmko/iStock; 22T, © DOC WHITE/Nature Picture Library; 22M, © Gerald Corsi/iStock; 22B, © Ajit S N/Shutterstock; 23TL, © User10095428_393/iStock; 23TR, © Michael Gomes/iStock; 23BL, © vm/iStock; 23BR, © FtLaudGirl/iStock.

See BearportPublishing.com for our statement on Generative AI Usage.

Library of Congress Cataloging-in-Publication Data

Names: Berne, Emma Carlson, 1979- author.
Title: Underwater animals / by Emma Carlson Berne.
Description: Minneapolis, Minnesota : Bearport Publishing Company, [2025] |
  Series: A watery world | Includes bibliographical references and index.
Identifiers: LCCN 2023059639 (print) | LCCN 2023059640 (ebook) | ISBN
  9798889169901 (library binding) | ISBN 9798892324595 (paperback) | ISBN
  9798892320955 (ebook)
Subjects: LCSH: Aquatic animals--Juvenile literature.
Classification: LCC QL120 .B38 2025 (print) | LCC QL120 (ebook) | DDC
  591.76--dc23/eng/20240123
LC record available at https://lccn.loc.gov/2023059639
LC ebook record available at https://lccn.loc.gov/2023059640

Copyright © 2025 Bearport Publishing Company. All rights reserved. No part of this publication may be reproduced in whole or in part, stored in any retrieval system, or transmitted in any form or by any means, electronic, mechanical, photocopying, recording, or otherwise, without written permission from the publisher. Bearport Publishing is a division of Chrysalis Education Group.

For more information, write to Bearport Publishing, 5357 Penn Avenue South, Minneapolis, MN 55419.

Contents

Dive In 4

Big Blue Whales 22

Glossary 23

Index 24

Read More 24

Learn More Online 24

About the Author 24

Dive In

Colorful fish swim by a large turtle.

A crab walks along the sand below.

The water is full of life!

Many animals live in rivers and lakes.

Small fish swim in these fresh waters.

Tiny tadpoles live there, too.

7

Bigger animals live in the ocean.

Sharks live in this salty water.

All underwater animals need many of the same things.

All animals need **oxygen**.

Most animals on land breathe it in.

How do underwater animals get it?

Some go above the water to breathe.

Most fish get oxygen a different way.

They have **gills**.

Water moves over their gills.

These slits take in oxygen.

Underwater animals need to eat, too.

They may munch on plants.

Some eat other animals.

Blue whales suck up small shrimp as they swim.

15

Many underwater animals move around to get food.

Most fish swim using their **fins**.

Sea stars crawl on many little legs.

Animals need different kinds of bodies for underwater life.

Some have fur that keeps them warm.

Sharp **spikes** or hard shells help some animals stay safe.

Lots of animals swim and live under water.

They get the things they need in different ways.

Look below the waves!

What animals do you see?

Big Blue Whales

Blue whales live in the oceans. They are the biggest animals on Earth!

Blue whales need to eat a lot. They chow down on thousands of shrimp every day.

Blue whales breathe air. They take it in from a hole on the top of their heads.

Blue whales have a lot of fat under their skin. It helps keep them warm.

22

Glossary

fins flaplike body parts that fish use to swim

gills body parts that help some animals breathe under water

oxygen something in air and water that is needed for animals to stay alive

spikes hard, sharp points

Index

fins 16
fur 18
gills 12–13
shells 18
spikes 18
swim 4, 6, 14, 16, 20

Read More

Caprioli, Claire. *Just Discovered Fish (Learn about: Animals)*. New York: Children's Press, 2024.

Sexton, Colleen. *Whales (Amazing Ocean Life)*. Minneapolis: Kaleidoscope, 2022.

Learn More Online

1. Go to **www.factsurfer.com** or scan the QR code below.
2. Enter "**Underwater Animals**" into the search box.
3. Click on the cover of this book to see a list of websites.

About the Author

Emma Carlson Berne lives with her family in Cincinnati, Ohio. Muskrats are her favorite underwater animals.